Once Upon A Summertime

From a child's diary of early Ponte Vedra summers

Illustrated and written by
Marion Whatley Cowart

This is a true story of a child's summer at a real location
as remembered and recorded in her diary. The book was
printed in the United States.

Book Designer: Alfred B. Ilagan

To order additional copies of this book, contact:
Xlibris Corporation
1-888-795-4274
www.Xlibris.com
Orders@Xlibris.com

Muffet, during the 1930's at Ponte Vedra Beach when she first started writing in her diary, a little red leather one with its own lock and key.

The author has followed the original diary journal entries and with her recollections has brought to life the summertime that she cherished.

The script is true, the memories still strong today and the illustrations are Muffet's very own.

And, as she says, the story is for beach children of all ages.

Dedicated to my grandchildren:
Emily, Will, Harlan, Emerson and Tyler
and other beach children of all ages.

FORWARD

Once upon a Summertime is a true accounting of a child's diary of PonteVedra Beach summers during the 1930's — a personal recollection and glimpse of a leisurely old fashioned way of life, that is quite unlike the fast paced computerized world of today the year 2000.

It all started quite fast. I walked into the dining room one morning for breakfast, and to my surprise, everyone was there. Dad, with a calmer-than-usual look; Brownie, with a curious sparkle in his eyes; and Mother, with a nervous smile. Then it came…. her big announcement; "Guess what sweetie? We have a surprise for you, now that you are a big girl. You are going on a trip to the hospital to have your tonsils out and that means NO SCHOOL TODAY! Now, isn't that nice?"

I froze for a moment on the edge of the chair then jumped up with feet flying to the front door, down the steps, across the front yard lickety-split through the neighbor's yard to the corner, hearing my father's voice and his feet pounding behind me.

Around the block I flew and, in a panic, returned to the backyard to my favorite, tall Chinaberry tree. I climbed to the tippy top with the limbs waving in the air. Unfortunately, this particular tree waved in the breeze by my big brother's window. He started yelling that he would chop down my favorite tree … with ME in it….. if I did not come down and return to the house.

I had struck out. Out of breath, home again and …. hello hospital.

At the hospital a few days later with a very sore throat, I over heard Dr. Boone, tell mother "Muffet has had too many colds and sore throats this winter. And what she really needs is" . . . oh no, here it comes more operations, big needles and yucky medicine. I couldn't believe my ears. . . "the fresh, salty sea air …… *at the beach*." The **BEACH**?

Holy jehosafat, I must be dreaming.

June

The cottage is quiet and it's early in the morning. I am looking out of my tiny bunk bed window toward the beach. A brown and white cow is looking in the window at me. How strange.

Mother comes into the bunkroom in her bathrobe and tells me "That's what these cows do. Eat our grass"! It's open range here and the cattle meander from Palm Valley over to the ocean and up the beach. Then they find our nice green lawn to munch. Flowers, too.

I think to myself, this place is sure different from living in town. No cows there. A strange awakening after my first night at the beach this summer!

Our new summer cottage is in Ponte Vedra Beach, Florida – and our family will stay right here 'til school starts in September.

Right here with the cows.

I am excited. I love this place already. With Mother and Dad we had watched this cottage being built all this past winter, coming here as we did on Saturdays and Sundays to inspect the progress.

Our cottage is one story, white wood with pink shutters. Mother calls this color 'shocking pink' after her SHOCKING PINK CHAPIRELLI PERFUME. Don't ask me why.

There are already beds of pink petunias around the yard plus beds of yellow, orange, purple, red and − guess what − *PINK* zinnias. Mother loves flowers and, as I have just learned, so do the fuzzy eared cows.

The reason I'm telling you all this is because the other day my father suggested I start a diary this summer and draw pictures as I go along. Well I can't write too well but I do draw. So this is my first diary entry so far.

Now I'm going swimming in my new bathing suit. It is blue and mostly white with a blue sailboat. It is made of thin sheet rubber. A new fashion I think.

June

A couple of days have gone by – mostly swimming – and now today I'm sunburned all over and so is my brother, Brownie, who is older. Mother has covered us with white Noxema cream and we look like dried pastry dough figures. We are to stay out of the sun for several days, says Mother.

Late last summer we did visit at the beach, staying in a cottage near the Ponte Vedra post office and The Store. Not so much sunburn then. But we did see and learn a lot about the ocean, the beach, shells, plants and all the little creatures that live here with us. Dad showed us purple jellyfish, starfish, pieces of coral, fiddler crabs, porpoises, sand pipers, osprey, possums, pelicans, sheepshead, sea urchins, sand dollars, Mayport fishing boats and most beautiful of all, the full moon at high tide.

At the first cottage we started collecting seashells. There were several big blustery, windy days – "nor'easter", according to Dad, that came along and brought bunches of brown seaweed ashore and lots of shells. Big rippling sloughs of wet sand were carved by the tide on the beach leaving small ponds of seawater trying to run furiously back to the low tide line. We saw no cows that summer.

About our new cottage: Inside the cottage all the walls are beautiful smooth cypress wood with unfinished white pine floors. All the beds – there are ten – are bunks built out of cypress wood onto the floor, with big drawers underneath to hold blankets and pillows, all sort of ship-like. There are double-decker bunks in our room. The cypress bureaus are tall with seven drawers and brass knobs, also built down to the floor.

The pine floors are so cool. I mean *really* smooth and cool. Bud scrubs all the floors every Monday with soap and water and Clorox. You just can't imagine how they feel with bare feet. It's like walking on satin.

There's a 30-foot-long, thickly padded window seat covered in royal blue canvas, stretching across the living room under the windows which overlook the ocean. Opposite the window seat is a huge almost-walk-in fireplace of soft-red brick with wide bookcases of cypress inset on each side. Pale yellow wood Venetian blinds fill all the windows helping to cool down the sun rays and let in the balmy breezes. On the big screen porch hangs a colorful velvety soft hammock in a corner, which everyone tries to claim at any given moment.

The only decorations on the walls in the cottage are Winslow Homer watercolor prints of the Bahamas, which are beautiful to look at and think about because they are pictures of real places by the sea. "A fine watercolorist" says my father.

A week ago in the morning a little moving van pulled to a stop in the oyster-shell driveway next door. Dad went across the yard to talk to the man who drove up behind the van. Another car came up behind the first and out jumped three girls and a lady. The tallest girl looked, to me, my age.

It was thus that my new to-be best friend, Cornelia, came into my life with her little sisters, Frances and Jane. My summer suddenly became peopled with a whole new special family and for the first time I didn't need to play baseball with the boys. My new best friend and I can now play jacks, hopscotch, jump-rope and cut out paper dolls to our hearts content all summer long.

Our parents – Cornelia's and mine – are already good friends. Cornelia's father is Dad's lawyer and 'Big Cornelia', her mother, loves to crab like my Mother. All four parents share afternoon terrace visits with one another. Often during these visits Cornelia and I are *encouraged* to entertain little Frances who is four, doing somersaults, singing nursery songs and playing patty-cake. Frances enjoys this probably less than we do. A good baby-sit most always brings a spend-the-night privilege for us, the nursemaids, so we carry on.

Soon after this beach summer began, the sun rose on my older brother's birthday, June 22nd. Brownie is eleven today and he wants nothing more than a surfboard. "No party, no cake, no ice-cream, no other presents," says he, boldly.

Once, some days ago, he saw a shiny blue plastic-covered balsa wood surfboard in Cohen Brothers department store in town and now he thinks of nothing else. At breakfast Dad goes out to his car, then returns with a huge brown paper-wrapped something. Suddenly Brownie was on his feet, up in the air, across the room with shouts of glee into Dad's arms, tearing off the brown paper. It was a you-know-what.

This afternoon Brownie, the surfboard and I were water bound for a long time. I have to say I am a tiny bit jealous. I actually had a turn or two on the board, not without a lot of do's and don'ts from the surfer. It really glides over the water like a sled on snow (as if I know *snow*).

As it turned out, there *was* birthday cake with candles and ice-cream too that night for desert. "Thank goodness" said hungry me.

After breakfast today the neighborhood gang explored the huge sand dune just south of the bulkhead ending. It looks to be three stories high from the beach side. We could see a wide wind-carved pathway right up the center to the top most point. There at the top is a flat area of pure white, soft sand hidden by a circle of low lying palmettos. This spot is to be our secret lookout fort that only a few of us explorers can know about.

Looking out over the palmettos back towards the cottage we could see Bud mowing the grass and the bathing suits flapping in the breeze on the clothesline.

Looking south along the wide beach, one could see only Barney's gas station/hamburger stand, and his ever-ready wrecker. Beyond, just dunes, palm trees and some tall magnolia trees with glistening green leaves. This view is like living on the edge of the earth with just the lonesome stretch of beach all the way to the horizon. No people, no houses. It must have looked like this when Ponce de Leon stepped ashore just south of here.

Today I am going to write about my parents.

During the summer Dad still goes to work everyday in the city. He does Real Estate (which means land) and builds houses and plans neighborhoods. That's how Ponte Vedra became a village around the little post office and The Store. He likes to draw and paint also.

Mother takes care of us all – first, Dad then Brownie and me, second and third (I'm third only in age).

Mother loves to play golf and occasionally lets me walk around the course with her, quietly. She reads a lot and keeps us and her in books from India Wood's Bookstore in the city. She always welcomes our friends to the cottage and plans fun things to do. Sometimes on weekends all of us children and our parents play ball and have cookouts.

Dad is our taskmaster and keeps Brownie and me on the job and our toes. Besides swimming laps at the new pool each day there is room cleaning every morning, washing the three cocker spaniels every Friday at the garage sink and carrying in the groceries everyday. Brownie runs a mile each morning, helps Bud mow the lawn, sweeps sand out of the cars and helps Bud churn the ice cream. As for me, I sew buttons on clean clothes in need, put up everyone's ironed clean clothes on Thursday, match pairs of clean socks, set the dinner table and weed the zinnia flower beds. We do not get an allowance, so you can bet we keep up our jobs, and goodwill to fund our needs. Dad, *The Foreman*, accepts *No Excuses* and that is that.

Today we are going to our first swimming lesson. We both swim – stay afloat – but "need to learn the proper form" says Dad. The Ponte Vedra Bath Club is now open this summer and Mother tells us that Helen Wainwright is our new swim coach. We learned that she is an Olympic Medalist (with the backstroke). I am excited to meet her.

A week goes by with lessons and practice every morning at nine at the pool. Ms. Wainwright is a good teacher and makes us try hard. She is quite a little person, slender, very tanned and wears a two-piece swim suit and white swim cap with her sunglasses perched on top of her head. Today she took off her swim cap and her dark brown hair fell almost to her knees. When she swam for us at the end of the lesson she just slithered through the water with barely a ripple.

Still swimming 12 laps every day. The new pool is beautiful and seems so long especially when we are on practice lap number one. Before driving to work Dad often stops by to check on us. "What lap are you on?" says he. He doesn't fool me one little bit and I sure don't try to fool him. *No Sir-ree!*

Our last challenge at the end of our swimming lessons just stunned me. Ms. Wainwright told us that it would be good if we would take a dive off the diving board, *the high one*, as our final exam. I had never even climbed up there. Brownie did well. But I was almost overcome with fright. I did it but I can now say (for the first time, out loud, so to speak) that it was too scary for words.

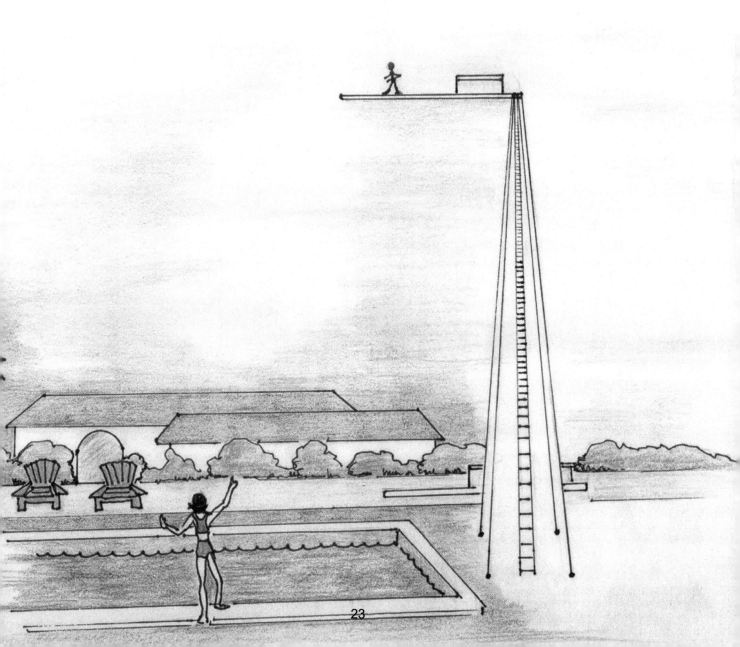

More about the new pool:

All around the pool (the adult pool, as it is called) is a wide brick walkway, on the edge of which are Adirondack chairs painted bright red, orange, yellow, green or blue. Behind the chairs are stretches of green grass where you can lie down on a towel.

A small shallow baby pool is on the far side, the three diving boards at one end and a view of the ocean at the other. Tables with bright canvas umbrella tops are all around also. There's even a lifeguard, Sam, who knows just everybody and is real careful to stop us from running around the wet brick walkway. Sam blows his whistle often if you don't follow the rules. *I KNOW.*

Two important people in my life are Bud and Della. Let me tell you about them.

Ever since I was real little, they have lived with us in town, (Jacksonville) and at the beach where they have a bedroom and a bath each. Mother calls Bud our special houseman and Della, seventeen, our fantastic cook. They take care of Brownie and me while our parents are out of town or at parties during the evening. Bud is really shy and he chuckles a lot but I know he means business when he directs us.

Della tries to be stern and makes her forehead frown when I don't do things just so – like sometimes when I leave my wet bathing suit on the shower floor, but she covers for me and doesn't tell.

Bud is a wonderful craftsman. He made our donax sieve that first summer. Donax? They are tiny little clams that are usually found on the water's edge, frantically digging themselves into the wet sand. Occasionally we will make donax soup which is as good as our imagination will allow, and also very salty and thin. When tasting it for the first time our houseguests politely say "Hm-m-m just delicious." I wonder about that.

When Bud and Della are not busy with the household and cooking tasks, they like to fish in the lagoon across the road behind the cottage. Brownie and I sometimes get to go with them. Usually we catch catfish.

This is what you do with catfish: Bud puts a catfish on a small board, drives a nail into it to hold it in place, then skins it, with the head off, covers it with flour and bread crumbs and fries it in the iron skillet. I have not yet acquired a taste for this delicacy.

During the summer in our new beach house we made our first trip to Mayport to crab on the docks. Mayport is a quaint little fishing village where all the commercial fishing boats unload their catch. Crabbing is fun but most often very hot, with no shade. Sun hats are a must as are sandals on the hot docks.

Mother loves crabmeat so she teaches us the way — first you cut long lines of heavy cord, tie cuts of old smelly raw meat onto one end, drop that end into the water along the dockside and secure the other end to the dock post.

It's easy to see the crabs in the shallow water as they attack the meat so we slip the long-handled crab net quietly into the water behind the crab and scoop up the creature. Today our catch was 31. "A good day's work," said Mother. She bought us each an ice cold Coca-Cola. That's unusual!

BLUE
CRAB

The best part of crabbing is back home again in the afternoon when Bud lights a fire under the big washtub of water in the yard, boils the crabs then cracks them open with a small hammer. Then we pick out the delicious meat. Eating crab with hot melted butter in the cool of the evening on the lawn is the way to go.

All the beach flowers are suddenly in bloom now. It's as though someone commanded: "Everybody bloom!" The colors are dazzling – even brilliant – and so unlike the pale, soft delicate colors of gardens in town. They must like the hot sand, the salt air, radiant sunlight and blustery breezes that surround them all summer long. I guess it makes them "hardy" as Mother, the garden person would say.

Along the bulkhead the pink railroad vine grows rampantly covering everything in sight. It looks like a rowdy relative of the delicate powder blue Morning Glory.

The Spanish Bayonet in bloom is a picture to behold. Dozens of creamy white ping-pong balls riotously balanced on one another in a three-foot cone shape atop the sharp pointed green swords.

Mother loves to bring home stalks of Sea Lavender and Goldenrod which grow profusely along the beach road. She fills the cottage with peppery bunches of them all even though they last for only several days.

A few beach beauties that my garden person has pointed out to me are the Purple Aster with its yellow button center, a black-eyed Susan, a yellow thistle, chicory with tiny blue flowers and a pink rugosa rose. The beach scene is extravagantly painted with their color and scents.

All things seem brighter and wilder and stronger. The sky at Ponte Vedra is bluer, breezes more constant, sun stronger and the soft white sand, warmer!

Everything is just . . . MORE!

Just like my beach memories will always be.

July

4th of July

The Fourth of July is upon us. Brownie and I, Cornelia, Tommy and the Saunders twins down the way, have planned to have a July 4th parade along the bulkhead in front of the cottages.

Dad bought us American flags, six in all. Parade dress would be whatever red, white or blue shirts and shorts we had.

We've been practicing a few songs for the event: "America the Beautiful", "My Country 'tis of Thee", "God Bless America", and the National Anthem, my favorite, as the finale. At the end of the parade we will recite the Pledge of Allegiance at my house. We printed notices of the event to hand out to our neighbors, which said:

> 10 AM Annual July 4th Parade
> on the Bulkhead

And we signed our names.

The parade was a big success! Everyone came out on the lawn to watch. We pledged the Allegiance at each house, not just mine. And all the families clapped after each patriotic song. At least the cows weren't around to moo us. *That's a joke.*

Dad and Bud shot Roman candles for everyone later that evening. Then we lay on the grass in the dark and watched the fireworks way up at Jacksonville Beach. The sky was filled with beautiful patterns like sparkling, dancing stars in full motion.

I thought about the very first Fourth of July when Francis Scott Key as a prisoner on a British ship wrote at dawn about "The rockets red glare, the bombs bursting in air, gave proof through the night that our flag was still there." How thrilling to think about this!

We have a special place along the beach that Dad named "the three palms". On weekends early in the morning Brownie and I often walk with Dad south of the cottage in the general direction of St. Augustine. Our three cocker spaniels, O'Shaunessy, Patrick O'Toole and Jezebel, are always with us to chase the sandpipers. Splashing in the water's edge, we walk past our secret sand dune fort, Barney's gas station/hamburger stand, the only two bits of civilization along the way. Two miles further along, the three palms rise up above the other vegetation in the dunes. This is always our final destination and turn-around spot.

When Dad started doing some serious oil painting, his first effort was the three palms. I love this painting and secretly hope to paint like this someday. I also secretly hope to own this painting to remind me of happy times if I were far away. I would hang it in my bedroom and go to sleep dreaming of the beach, the ocean and cool breezes.

This morning the family was up earlier than usual. It was so hot – Dad called from the terrace, "Come take a walk with me." And so we set off walking down the beach toward the three palms. Suddenly we saw further along a huge sea turtle emerge with effort from the surf and head slowly for the high tide line. "It's a mother turtle." said Dad. "And she's about to make a nest. We must not disturb her."

When she reached the dunes, she started digging into the soft sand with her flippers. Dad explained that she would deposit her eggs in a deep nest, then cover them carefully with sand and return to sea. So many days later the baby turtles would hatch, climb out of their nest and instinctively head for the ocean.

We watched for awhile at a distance so as not to frighten her then we walked quietly on. The only evidence of her coming ashore were her distinct "foot prints", the ruts that her flippers cut into the sand as she came in from the ocean. Just think: she would *never see her babies*. That was an exciting experience for me to see!

To my utter and complete surprise today we saw two cowboys on cow ponies galloping over the sand dunes and onto the beach. It was like a Wild West movie scene. Continuing on past me, the cowboys raced toward the meandering cow herd which had passed by earlier. The riders wore cowboy hats, of course, jeans, boots with spurs, and carried lariats circling their saddle horns. The cowboys surrounded the herd, finally turning them south again on the beach. The fuzzy-eared ones moved listlessly along mooing, as the men shouted their ye-haws and giddy-ups.

Again Mother enlightened us with an explanation "This is what cows and cowboys do when the animals roam too far from the ranch."

But it just seemed weird, here at the beach. They should have exited singing, "Just an ol' cowhand on the Rio Grande."

Later in the day Cornelia and I took peanut butter sandwiches, bananas and bottles of chocolate milk to the fort for lunch. After that, back at the cottage we played jacks and then swam with Brownie and the neighbors.

The Japanese Shop is our latest discovery on First Avenue. Brownie and I found this place the day Mother parked her car right in front of it at Jacksonville Beach. She had asked us to stick close by the car until her grocery shopping was done. The ever-so-intriguing objects in the shop window, colorful parasols, kimonos, kites and posters enticed us to enter so we did just that. The owners, a Japanese couple dressed in bright red and yellow kimonos came forward with their hands clasped in front of them smiling – welcoming us with a slight bow. We bowed back to them not knowing what else to do or say.

They proceeded to remove objects from the display cases to show us: wooden boxes with secret openings, wood puzzles, Japanese dolls with pale faces and coarse, stiff black hair, chess set figures, chopsticks, watercolor posters, jade animals, oriental beads and much, much more.

As we continued to investigate each display item, tinkling wind chimes and the couple's soft musical voices could be heard in the background. We tried to whisper as we discussed prices and the thousands of treasures.

The only purchase that I could afford after a second round of looking was a small pink clamshell, which in water opens up, sending a pink paper lily on a string to the surface. This action unfortunately happens only once. Brownie would not make a single purchase…he tends to hang onto his money. I am forever the big spender. I am sure however that the tiny little exotic shop will draw us back again on other visits over the summer – costly visits for me probably.

Maybe I should start sweeping the terrace and the walkway regularly.

The seiners come every afternoon in good weather. They came today. We always race down to the ocean edge to watch them and to help (so we think) picking seaweed, crabs and shells out of their net on the shore.

I believe the families who work the nets live in Palm Valley. They come usually with their whole family in a Model T Ford right onto the beach with the heavy nets lying crosswise on the back of the auto. There are six or so men seining with two taking one end of the net out through the surf, beyond the breakers then making a horseshoe circle back onto shore. Then out of the water, all the way come the nets. Fish are frantically trying to jump out of the net to their freedom and there is much splashing about with the men shouting directions at one another. A good catch might produce 25 to 40 mullet each run and the men might seine there for an hour. You can generally see the schools of fish moving along the surface of the water so the seiners are alert to move out fast with the nets.

My Dad, Cornelia's dad and another neighbor father purchased our very own seine net. It's a little smaller in length than the one belonging to the Palm Valley fisherman – but just the right size for us all to pull. So now we can catch our own fresh seafood for the regular weekend fish fry on the beach. We also got a very small minnow seine with very small mesh to catch bait for pole fishing and crabbing. "We're in business now," says Dad.

This morning I cleaned the dust from around my shell collection. My shells are displayed on bookcase shelves on each side of the fireplace. I am so proud of my growing collection and hope someday to make a big classroom display at school. Mother brought me a shell handbook of Florida seashells so I'm learning their true names – not just their common names like "Jingle Shell" or "Baby's Foot" or "Turkey Wing". I love their beautiful soft colors: pale yellow, orange, pink and lavender and the many different and unusual shapes and sizes.

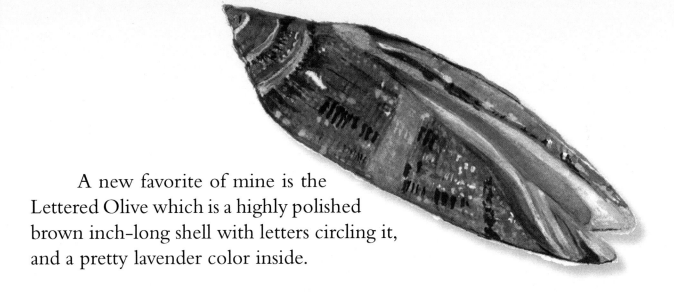

A new favorite of mine is the Lettered Olive which is a highly polished brown inch-long shell with letters circling it, and a pretty lavender color inside.

My all time favorite forever is the pink Scallop and I will always remember finding the first one. It is hard to believe that these shells were the homes of animals that lived on the ocean floor.

This afternoon, as I was about to float off to dreamland in the porch hammock, I spotted Bud carrying the wash tub (formerly the crab boil tub) to the terrace. Low and behold, the tub had a hunk of ice in it. That means only one thing! Brownie suddenly appeared with a huge watermelon in his arms. And with that, Mother abruptly shows up asking me to "invite the neighborhood children over". (The neighborhood children are better known to members as "the gang". It sounds more like us.)

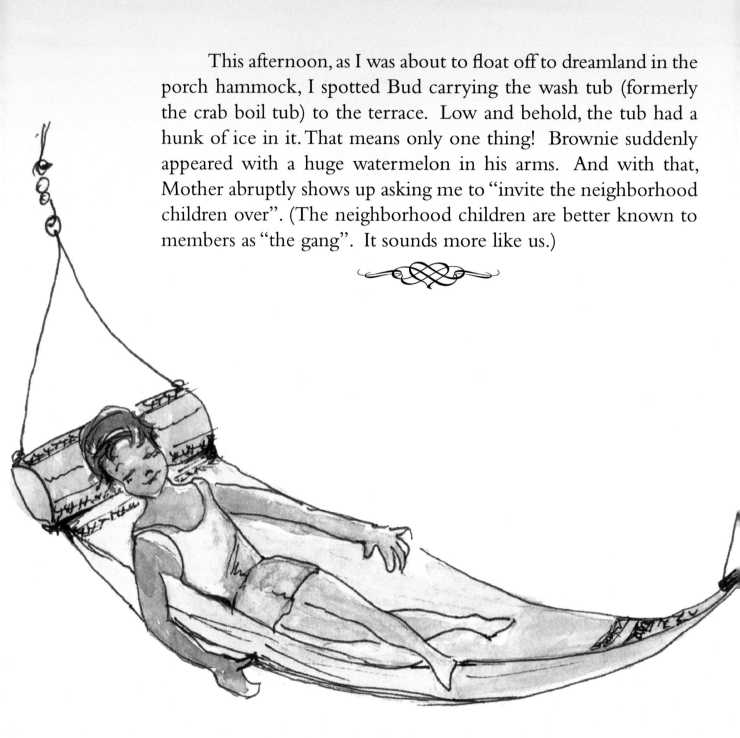

So just like that we were having a watermelon feast! The watermelon is a regular happening at our house but mother always surprises us with her timing. Bud cuts big slices which we all take to the bulkhead where we have a contest to see who can spit the watermelon seeds the farthest. Sometimes we even put on our swim suits so we can clean up afterwards in the ocean. Watermelon juice is sticky.

Watermelon – how can I say it – is maybe the second best to peach ice cream, but simply de-licious.

Our cousins from Baltimore are arriving tomorrow for a summer visit with us at the cottage. Brownie and I are really happy! Patsy, who is Brownie's age, Ginny Lee, in high school and Kay who is engaged and wears (I am told) Whit's heavy crest ring as her engagement ring.

Aunt Kathryn, their mother is bringing them by steamship, down the coast to Jacksonville. How exciting that must be!

Mother drives Brownie and me to the Jetties – that's where the St. John's River flows out to sea. "The steamship will enter the mouth of the river (at the jetties) about three P.M. en route to the steamship docks in town", says Mother. So we climb the huge gray jetty boulders to see the ship and wave, hoping they will see us. Then back to the car to drive into town to greet them.

Our three girl cousins are pretty, but they are very pale-skinned in their bathing suits. Brownie and I feel like brown crusty raisins and country bumpkins next to them in their dainty dresses, hair ribbons, shoes and all.

Aunt Kathryn is very fair with green eyes and she wears a sun hat, carries a parasol and long sleeves to cover her arms. She hardly looks like Mother's sister. Mother has dark hair and eyes and very sun tanned skin.

Since their arrival we have been swimming every day early. We stay at the beach until about 11 A.M., then back to the cottage for lunch. After lunch there is rest hour in the bunkroom with the sea breezes gently rattling through the bunkroom blinds. No one ever complains about rest time. We read – for me it's the *Bobbsey Twins* series, Brownie, his latest *Popular Science* magazine and for the cousins, following their Roland Park Country Day School reading list, *The Secret Garden and Jane Eyre.* Kay, of course, is always into her daily love letter from Whit. *La-di-dah!*

Tonight's dinner with our cousins calls for homemade ice cream. We all voted for peach, and so Bud and Brownie retreated to the garage, packing the wooden churn with ice and salt. Della had made the cream with fresh peaches and all the rest of us hang around waiting to have a taste, greedily spooning off the ice cream from the dipper.

Let me tell you now about dinner time.

In the living/dining room is a beautifully crafted natural cypress wood table that is eight feet long with stout pegged legs. The table top itself is two inches thick. A cypress bench designed exactly like the table stretches along one side of the table with the window seat for seating along the other side. Dad sits at the head, with Mother on his right on the bench and Brownie on his left on the window seat. I sit beside Mother with our guests, when present, all mixed in and around.

There's always lots to talk about (besides table manners) and always Della's cooking to enjoy. But best of all is desert…ice cream being top prize. I'm always first through dinner but Bud does not serve me dessert until everyone else has finished also. (It's really hard to just sit there and wait.)

Sometimes in the evening around dinnertime the land breezes set in — which means an army of gnats and bugs emerge from the lagoon behind us. They squeeze right through the window screens and completely cover all the lamps and the light bulbs — so bad sometimes that we have to turn off all the lights and spray the cottage with "Quick Henry the Flit", which smells like kerosene.

After dinner all the grownups sit out on the terrace while we play Monopoly at the big table. I generally go bankrupt first. (Spending money as usual).

I have two grandmothers that I dearly love. Grandmother Harlan often visits us from town. She has a shiny black Packard touring car that has foldout jump seats for me and my brother. She also has a chauffeur named James. When Grandmother comes to take us for an afternoon ride, James puts us in the jump seats and we say "Home James!" Then we just die laughing. I guess we saw that in some movie. James drives the Packard onto the beach at Jacksonville Beach, and then drives south to the cottage at Ponte Vedra. It's important to watch the tide and the time of day so the car doesn't get stranded by an incoming tide. We drove by our secret sand dune fort one day and pointed it out to Grandmother. She promised not to give away our secret hideaway and, she crossed her heart saying she wouldn't tell a soul.

Grandmother Whatley is an artist and paints lovely portraits. She also sews lovely things and makes my sun suits, when she visits. She has deep cornflower blue eyes and smiles a lot. Last summer she made a bathing suit for me. And was that ever funny!

She made it two-piece with blue wool. On the first day in my new suit we had company and I was looking forward to showing it off. As I dove into a wave and surfaced my suit started stretching longer and longer, way down to my knees. It became very heavy with seawater…so soggy in fact that I had to squeeze out the water in order to stand up and struggle back to the cottage to change. I showed it off all right! "The wrong kind of wool", said Grandmother later, "no more custom made bathing suits". "Right, Grandmother," said I!

August

It's already August and I am surprised!

Coming to the end of summer makes me wish for its beginning in June … That special moment when we drive to the beach with a carload of suitcases, groceries and three cocker spaniels. The trip seems endless; we are restless and impatient to arrive – and suddenly we cross the little bridge at Pablo Creek and see the vast beautiful stretch of green marshes ahead.

The salt air and the pungent vegetation are abruptly upon me. Even blindfolded, I would know the beach is minutes away and summertime awaits me. As Grandmother Harlan says, "The best is yet to come."

That's why August always surprises me…It sneaks up unexpectedly and reminds me that just 31 days remain before we go back to town to school. And….shoes.

I will try hard not to think about all that right now.

Our cousins had never ever had fresh figs before! Can you imagine that? So we all decided another trip to Mayport was in order. During fig season, which is now, a Mayport family with an enormous house-size fig tree, sells fresh figs in quart baskets from their side porch. The cousins enjoyed actually seeing the huge fig tree and we all helped carry many quart baskets of fat, juicy, purple figs to Mother's car, for the trip back to the beach cottage.

That night for dessert we had fresh figs sliced on saltine crackers spread with Philadelphia Cream Cheese. We ate a bundle! Then the next morning, guess what? Sliced fresh figs with cream for breakfast! Like watermelon and peach ice cream, just delicious! Mother and Della are now guarding the remaining figs with an eagle eye.

On our way home from the Mayport fig trip, we drove by the Jean Ribault Monument, to show it to the cousins. It tells about the 16th century French explorer who tried to claim the land around the St. John's River for France. He had sailed into the mouth of the river on May Day, (May 1) and named it "the River May". (This is also how Mayport got its name.)

Maxie is our neighborhood iceman who arrives each morning at the kitchen door in his tan uniform with his red ice tongs hooked into and around a huge fifty pound block of ice. He casually swings it into our icebox then happily greets everyone present. To me he says, "Good morning Miss Muffet who sits on a tuffet" and then laughs like he just told the best joke!

One day Maxie was making his regular delivery to our neighborhood when apparently the brakes slipped as his ice truck rumbled lickity-split up to the garage. Maxie and the ice truck went crash-bang through the other side of the garage and bumpity-bump down the front yard with blocks of ice flying hither and yon.

Maxie and the truck finally stopped at the ocean's edge. Everyone's ice was scattered along the wild path of the wandering ice truck.

A few blocks of ice floated out to sea. The price of ice must have gone up drastically that day and all of Ponte Vedra's iceboxes warmed up considerably. Our Jell-O melted. It's a wonder the Journal reporter didn't show up – the cows did, however and they seemed to enjoy licking their unexpected and curiously large treats.

I sat for a long while with Maxie on his running board waiting for the tide to recede and the wrecker to dislodge the truck wheels in the wet sand. Finally Maxie regained his courage and charged back up the yard and through the gaping hole in the garage.

Maxie was back on the job the next day with his full size grin and a jovial "Morning" to everyone. He is still driving lickety-split but with new brakes and a veteran's confidence at the wheel. Hurray! The iceman!

Marineland, the salt-water aquarium south of St. Augustine is open to the public this summer. Mother is taking us – cousins and all – there for the day. We leave at 10:00 A.M. with a huge picnic basket of fried chicken which Della fried earlier. Apple pie also.

In route we drive down the beach highway past the scary old ruins of an early rum runner's hideaway nestled secretly in among the sand dunes, past roadsides covered in sea oats, goldenrod, purple sea heather and kudzu vines, past long lines of pelicans sweeping gracefully over the palm trees. Ft. Marion soon appeared beyond the Vilano Bridge, then the gates of St. Augustine, the oldest school house, the slave market and finally the Bridge of Lions. We take lots of pictures of Patsy, Ginny Lee and Kay for their scrapbook, along the way.

It's already hot and the tourist crowd is large. At the ticket box at Marineland we meet Pete, the parrot, who is wildly swinging on his perch. He is a beautiful shade of green with yellow flecks of color on his wing and a red head. Boy, does he ever talk! In a loud voice, he screeches "Hello, kid" and "One for the money", over and over again.

The large aquarium tank, two stories high and big as a house, is filled with thousands of bright rainbow-colored fish of all sizes and shapes. There is a diver who makes a regular appearance underwater with a big net basket of fish food which he tosses out to the fish.

As I look through the glass portholes at the fish, they are often at the window looking back at me. I wonder what they must think!

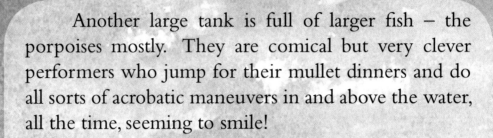

Another large tank is full of larger fish – the porpoises mostly. They are comical but very clever performers who jump for their mullet dinners and do all sorts of acrobatic maneuvers in and above the water, all the time, seeming to smile!

Yesterday, the two men in sailor suits who conduct the porpoise show asked me … me! … to feed the porpoises. I was instructed to walk out on a little bridge above the water with one sailor beside me, holding a bucket of mullet. The sailor lowered a large brass bell on a chain down into the tank and rang it under water. Dinnertime! With that the porpoises jumped and dove like crazy, splashing around in the water. I threw the mullet into the air and those slick creatures skimmed through the water jumping and catching their dinner without a miss, each time.

I had my picture taken at the bridge and was given a certificate with my name written on it, as "Jump Master for the Day". My brother said I'd be on the front page of the Journal but Mother said he was just joking. Darn! (I really think he is jealous.)

We are not allowed to buy swim floats, water wings, inner tubes or rafts for use in the ocean. As Dad said, "Such devices can let you drift out to sea in no time at all. It is important to be a strong swimmer and depend on yourself." He's right of course.

We did however invent a homemade pillowcase float unbeknownst to you-know-who. Snitching two pillow cases from the linen closet, then racing to the ocean, we filled the pillowcases with the sea breeze, gathering the open end tightly together and pulling it down into the water slightly. The upper part of the cases would billow out and off we'd float, hanging on to the puffy pillowcases.

We could float to the Bath Club in record time. Finally, when *you-know-who* learned of our sneaky device, he forgave us since we were becoming strong swimmers and knew about the treacherous undertow. He said also and, I proudly quote, "That pillowcase is quite an invention".

Our trip to Marineland was such a treat that we all begged Mother to take us and the cousins back down the way to St. Augustine "the oldest city in America", for a history trip. Mother happily agreed (she was sort of out numbered!)

So we set out to plan the event in advance. Each of us, we decided, would choose a special place to visit and the order of the visit. We had a tourist map to go by.

Patsy, the horse lover, voted for a horse and carriage to take us about the city. Kay wanted a drink from the Ponce de Leon Fountain of Youth; Ginny Lee, a visit to the oldest house; Brownie, the Wax Museum and the Ponce de Leon statue at the Bridge of Lions; and I chose my "namesake" Ft. Marion.

So, with our plans in order, off we set with the picnic basket filled with Della's fried chicken and as she says "All the fixin's". We met our carriage driver at the foot of the San Marco Avenue and climbed aboard the carriage for the historic adventure. What fun we had! Charles, our driver was decked out in a top hat with tails and Nellie his grey mare wore a daisy-covered straw hat with ear holes. Down the avenue we clip-clopped past the city gates to the Fountain of Youth.

We did it all! And Nellie was as exhausted with the load as we were with the fun. We learned all about the Spanish, French and English explorers who all fought for possession of St. Augustine and the Timucuan Indians, the original native settlers.

We enjoyed Della's fried chicken on the grounds of the fort and it was there that my Mother told everyone the old familiar family joke about me being named for Ft. Marion. I actually believed this for a while as my Dad said it was so, even though my Mother is also Marion. Dumb me.

As the sun went down – we watched the sailboats returning to Matanzas Bay, homeward bound to the marina docks. It was a special day to remember – all about the early days of America.

My third grade teacher, Mrs. Jarvis, once taught our class that "necessity is the Mother of invention". (We were studying about the cotton gin.) It means when you need it, you make it.

A northeaster was churning up and we needed a beach sailing boat badly, to go with the wind on the hard packed sand. Brownie, engineer that he was, figured that my flexible flyer (which was on 4 wheels) when fitted with a sail would out race our beach buddies on their bikes. With that goal in mind, we began.

Bud gave us some old mop poles and Mother donated a worn-out bed sheet. Behold! We had a dandy sailboat with a spinnaker, on wheels. At low tide we could fly along at a mighty pace. Nobody but nobody could beat us. Ever again.

Today is vegetable day

Our vegetable man is a regular visitor to the neighborhood. He usually clangs by on Friday, ringing his bell announcing the items for sale that day. He grows vegetables in Palm Valley and then delivers and sells in Ponte Vedra. He has everything: watermelons, bananas, squash, greens, beans, tomatoes, potatoes, lettuce, and boiled peanuts.

All the bright colored vegetables are displayed in large clean baskets in the open bed of his truck. Hanging above the veggies at the back is a large scale and above it all is a homemade red and white striped awning to ward off the sun and rain.

When one hears the vegetable man, it's time to race out the kitchen door to wave him down. He has what we think is an Italian accent and it's hard for all of us to understand one another. So we do a lot of pointing at the vegetables and he does a lot of smiling because Della always has a big list. Then after the purchases he clangs away.

Today the dragonflies, which look like small double winged airplanes, are out in droves, so tonight will probably be a big bug night. Patsy and I are at the kitchen table dividing up some sea shells and Aunt Kathryn is packing up the cousins to leave for Baltimore in the morning. They will return by train. It's really sad to think how empty the bunkroom will be. No more scary ghost stories to share, no more serious Monopoly games, or ping-pong competitions, no more excursions round about, or surfing with the surfer.

So, for the last time together we make a trip to our secret and beloved sand dune fort for a special good-bye ceremony. We scramble up the dunes to the look out spot and each of us writes our initials in the sand with a stick. We promise to keep our secret location a secret forever and to return again together next year. Ginny Lee said "amen" and we stuck our sticks in the sand where we had placed some seashells in a circle pattern. Then sadly we trudged homeward down the beach.

A few days later, best friend, Cornelia and I were heading out to the beach late in the afternoon to play hopscotch, and guess what? I suddenly saw a long black winding path trailing to the water's edge. I realized that we were observing a line of millions (it seemed) of tiny turtle babies furiously toddling to the ocean.

Nothing detained them! The instant they reached the water their little flippers turned into swim fins flailing through the surf like miniature windmills instinctively set on a destination. I thought about another mother turtle just like theirs who would never see her babies return to sea.
At that moment I hoped these tiny creatures would reach safety in their new ocean home.

School starts tomorrow and Bud will drive us into town while Mother and Della pack. How sad to leave our little pink-shuttered cottage. And how hard to put on shoes.

Grandmother Whatley told me once that "memories sometimes fade with time". I hope not. But just in case, this diary will help to recall it all.

If I could bake a fortune cookie with a guaranteed come-true end for everyone, I would insert a message saying, "A glorious summer at Ponte Vedra is coming to you". Then I would be able to share my special summer-time good fortune and these memories forever.

I know at least, anyway, that the ocean waves will always be crashing onto the shore and three palms somewhere will be waving in the breeze and another walk along the lacey edge of the surf will be waiting here at Ponte Vedra for me, just the way it was.

I count my blessings.

ABOUT THE AUTHOR

Marion Whatley Cowart is a native Floridian, a life-long student of art with a lifetime love of the beach. She is the mother of two daughters and two sons, and is married to William Franklin Cowart, also a native Floridian, former resident of Jackson, Wyoming and past representative for the Hughes Aircraft Company, Paris France.

"Muffet" as she is called by her friends and grandchildren was born in Jacksonville, attended Bartram School and graduated from Goucher College, Baltimore, Maryland. Subsequently she worked for the State Department and lived in Georgetown. Later upon returning to her much loved Florida she established an advertising art business.

Now a full-time resident of Ponte Vedra (her childhood summer time home), she spends lots of time traveling with husband Bill and entertaining her happy bunch of five young grandchildren reading, telling stories and giving art lessons. She lives surprisingly enough on the exact spot where the three palms (in this book) once stood.

She is still collecting sea shells.